LEVERAGING ON INDIA - BEST PRACTICES RELATED TO MANUFACTURING, ENGINEERING AND IT

LEVERAGING ON INDIA - BEST PRACTICES RELATED TO MANUFACTURING, ENGINEERING AND IT

A Guide to the Western World

S. CHANDRASEKAR

PARTRIDGE
A Penguin Random House Company

ISBN: Softcover   978-1-4828-6709-1
             eBook   978-1-4828-6708-4

To order additional copies of this book, contact
Partridge India
000 800 10062 62
orders.india@partridgepublishing.com

www.partridgepublishing.com/india

What Is the Best Fit for India?

1. If your business is related to manufactured goods, the candidates that suit India well are labour-intensive, high-volume products. The commodities in this category are raw castings, machined castings, forgings (both raw and machined), fabrication parts, and industrial chains. The average labour rate in India is around two hundred US dollars per month for foundry work and three hundred US dollars per month for CNC machined parts. The extreme difference in wages between those of operators in India and those in the Western world make it a good starting point.

2. The consideration in development of Indian manufacturing suppliers is that their learning curves are very high compared to Western standards.

3. Another challenging factor is culture. Indian entrepreneurs do not deliver on promised delivery dates. There is always a factor of delay, which disappoints the Western customers. The Western community should factor in this aspect while working with Indian businessmen.

4. The bright side of business is that cost savings in buying from Indian suppliers remain intact but for the delay in the start-up of projects.

5. The next step after stabilizing the parts for products is to step up the value change and make the product or the assembly. As the factors of labour content and machining content, along with labour-intensive assembly, increase in the total output, the cost savings for the Western buyers increase, and also, the profits for the Indian manufacturers increase. This is a case of a perfect win-win situation.

6. One extra reason to do business with Indian suppliers is that they are committed to protection of intellectual property rights of the Western customers. As of today, no violation of IP has been reported.

7. Training for Best Practices
   One critical success factor for the project would be to train Indian operators and Indian executives in the premises and business environment of the related Western customers. The cost of training can be absorbed by the Indian companies.

8. As the operators are better trained and improve on the clarity of work, productivity will significantly improve. There will be high reduction in non-value-added activities and reduction in wastages and rejects. This will bring the overall cost down and profit margin up, which can be shared by both the Western and Indian companies.

9. Caution on Joint Ventures

If the Western counterpart is looking at joint ventures, cautionary advice will be as follows:

a. Start the relationship on a customer–supplier basis, and when the relationship is well established with respect to productivity, quality, and price, focus on joint ventures on refined methods as outlined below.

b. Here is a suggested portfolio for the joint venture model:

Period	Financial participation
Year 1	10%
Year 2	20%
Year 3	30%
Year 4	40%

A periodic dosage of funds based on results demonstrated and profits absorbed will mitigate the risk of a project failure and make the relationship more dynamic with 100 per cent OTD and zero defects.

10. The strategy of sourcing from an Indian manufacturer should be based on the concept of single-point sourcing—which means the supplier has all the related manufacturing equipment, machinery, tools, gauges, a pattern shop, and a metallurgical lab under one roof with no need for outsourcing. This strategy of single-point sourcing will help in the establishment of quality assurance procedures, best practices related to manufacturing, high productivity, zero defects, and very much reduced cost.

11. Engineering services—this is one of the major strengths of India. With more than three hundred thousand engineers graduating every year, there is abundant talent in a readily available condition as these young engineers are well exposed to engineering software and related applications. There are two methods of outsourcing engineering services—the first is on-site, and the second is offshore. In the on-site method, the Indian service provider deploys the number of engineers required to the relevant skill set and talent base at the premises of the customer to work under the supervision of Western managers. In the offshore method, the Indian service provider works with resources in Indian offices and generates delivery to their Western customers.

Proven best practices for communication and interaction are through conference calls.

12. With a selection of engineering service providers from among a few thousands of Indian firms available, the critical success factor here would be to work with large, globally proven players like Tata, Infosys, Infotech, and Wipro. These large companies have their presence all over the world, with the reach and spread to provide service at any point in the world. These firms have the successful experience of having executed multiple diverse engineering projects ranging from low-level difficulty to high-level difficulty. Cost saving on engineering project man hours would be a direct benefit for the Western customers. The practice for IT is very much the same as engineering.

For your specific queries, please address them to chandrew20022002@ yahoo.co.in.

The author, S. Chandrasekar, is an engineer and a charted financial analyst with twenty-six years of successful work experience with MNCs. The author is an alumnus of BITS Pilani and the Indian Institute of Management, Trichy.

What follows is a direct comparison between India and China—their strengths and weaknesses and how efforts should be focused to synergize and capture the best benefits for Western customers—in particular, MNCs.

    a.   India and China—an Overview

    b.   Project Scope

    c.   Economic Indicators

    d.   Sector-Wise Analysis

    e.   Challenges Faced

    f.   Proposed Reforms

Economic Policy

China	India
■ Methodical and deliberate	■ Chaotic and opportunistic
■ Transiting from an agricultural economy to a robust industrial economy	■ Transiting from an agricultural to a knowledge-based service economy
■ Industrial economy—employment for the rural areas and people with minimum education	■ Knowledge-based—this gives employment opportunities to the highly educated urban people
■ "Made in China"	■ BPO—creates no intellectual property for an Indian firm. Threat for these jobs to shift to other countries
■ State-of-the-art infrastructure	
■ FDI and domestic— backward and forward linkages	■ Absence of well-developed infrastructure (power and transportation)

Project Scope

a. Comparison of Indian and Chinese economies

b. Analysis of parameters that govern the economies

c. Present economic status of India and China, challenges faced

Key Economic Indicators

	China	India
Population (2010)	1,339,724,852	1,210,193,422
Population growth	0.5%	1.2%
GDP	$10.36 trillion (nominal, 2014 est.)	$2.308 trillion (nominal, April 2015)
	$17.63 trillion (PPP, 2014)	$7.996 trillion (PPP, April 2015)
GDP rank	2 (nominal)/1 (PPP)	7 (nominal)/3 (PPP)
GDP growth	9.5% (nominal, 2013) 7.4% (real, 2014)	11.5% (nominal, 2014–15) 7.4% (real, 2014–15)
GDP per capita	$8,211 (nominal, 82nd, 2014) $13,992 (PPP, 89th, 2014)	$1,808 (nominal, 131st, 2015) $6,265 (PPP, 121st, 2015)
GDP per sector	9.2% (agriculture) 42.6% (industry) 48.2% (service)	13.7% (agriculture) 21.5% (industry) 64.8% (service)
Inflation (CPI)	2.0% (2014)	5.1%
Population below poverty line	6.1% (2013)	23.6% (2011)
Labour force	787.6 million (2012)	487.3 million (2013 est.)
Unemployment	4.1% (Q2, 2014)	5% (NSSO method, 2013)
Average gross salary	$669 monthly (2012)	$130 monthly (2010)

GDP Per Capita—India and China

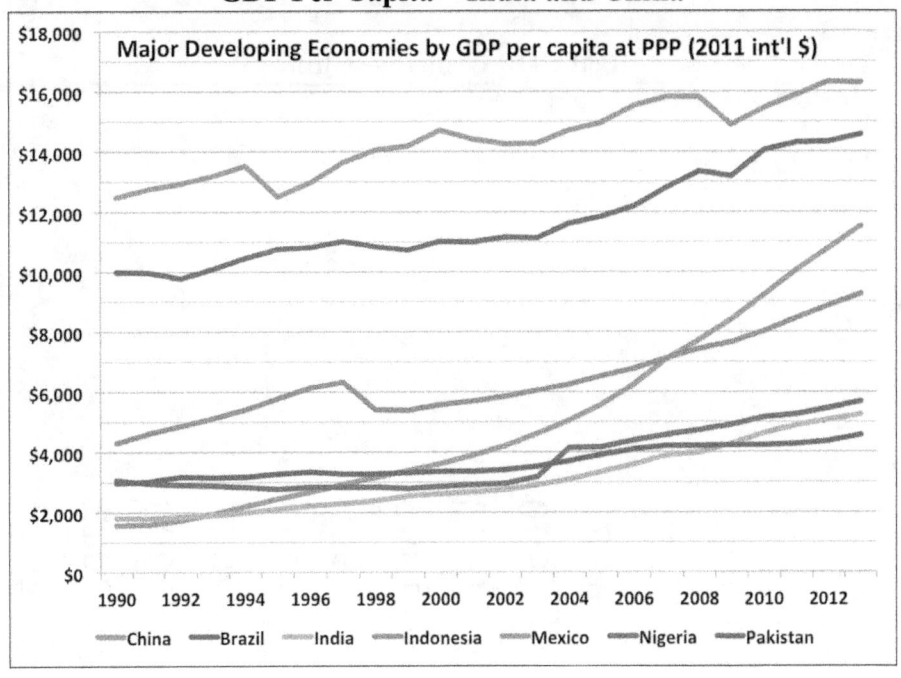

Major Developing Economies by GDP per capita at PPP (2011 int'l $)

China Brazil India Indonesia Mexico Nigeria Pakistan

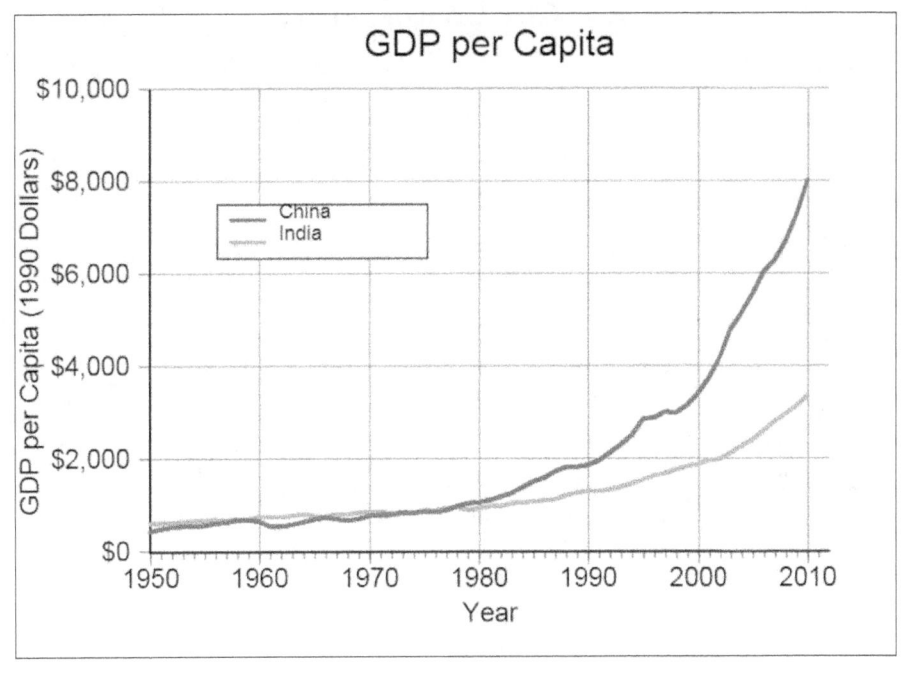

GDP per Capita

Real GDP Growth—China

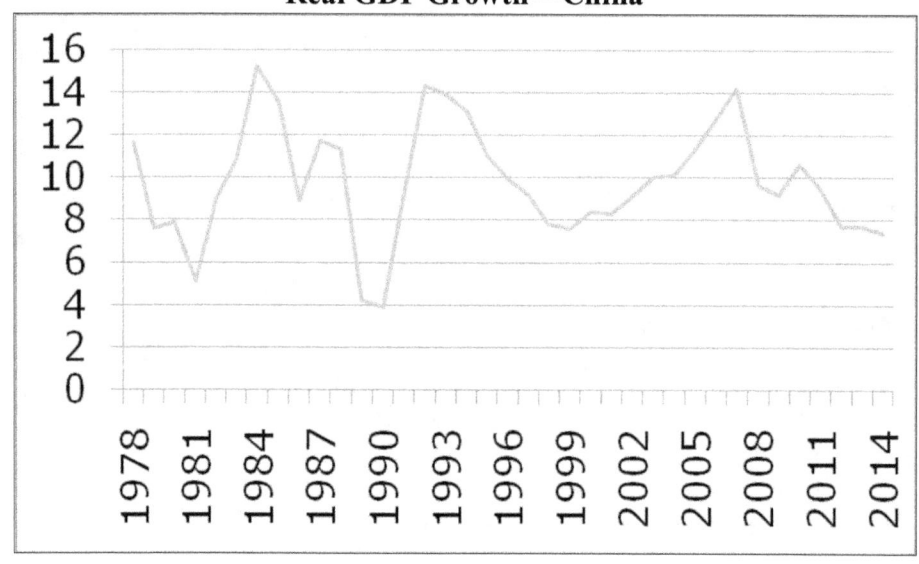

Real GDP Growth—India

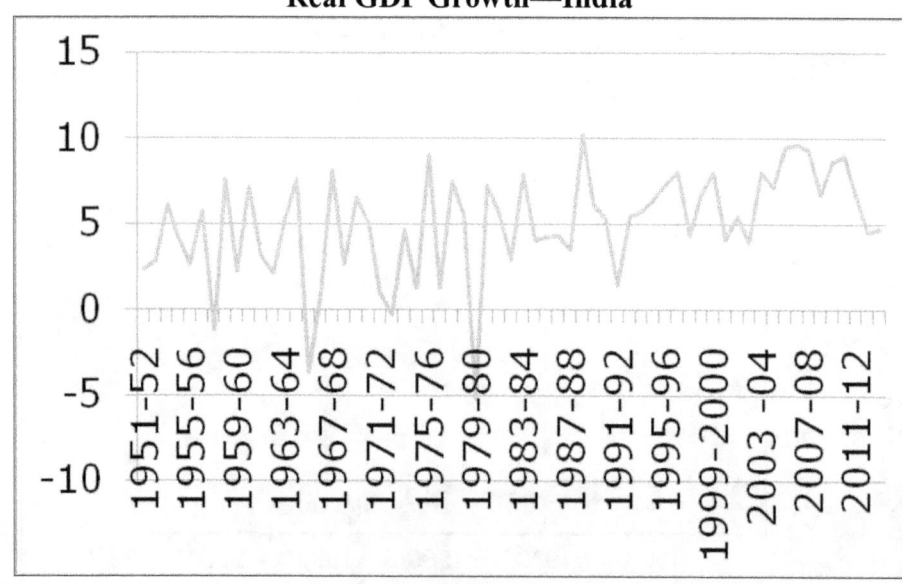

Economic Performance since Reform

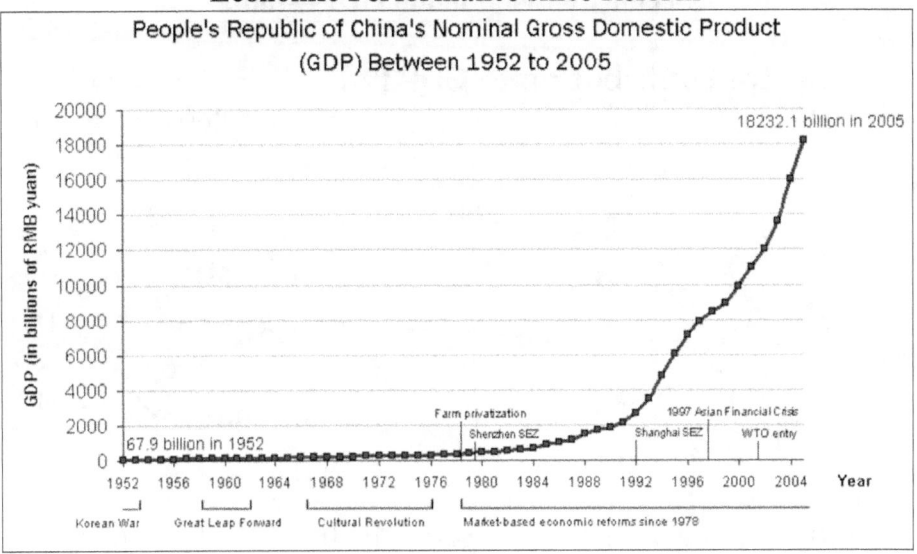

Economic Performance since Reform

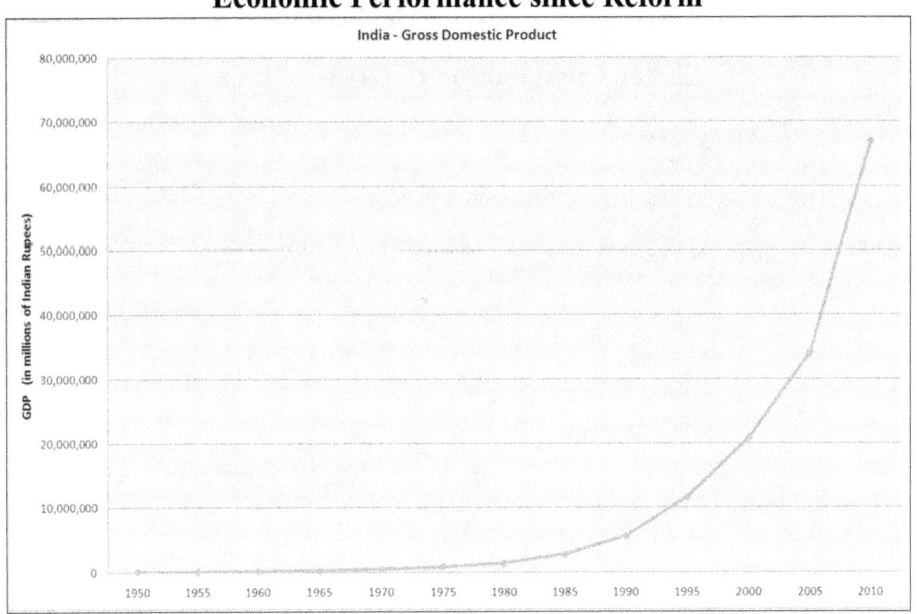

Sector Contribution to GDP—India

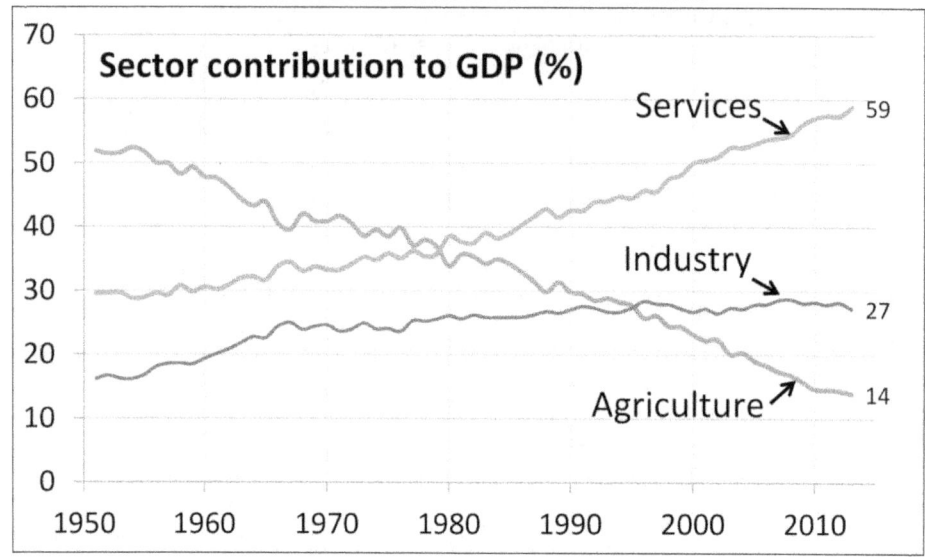

Sector contribution to GDP (%)

Services 59

Industry 27

Agriculture 14

1950 1960 1970 1980 1990 2000 2010

Sector Contribution to GDP—China

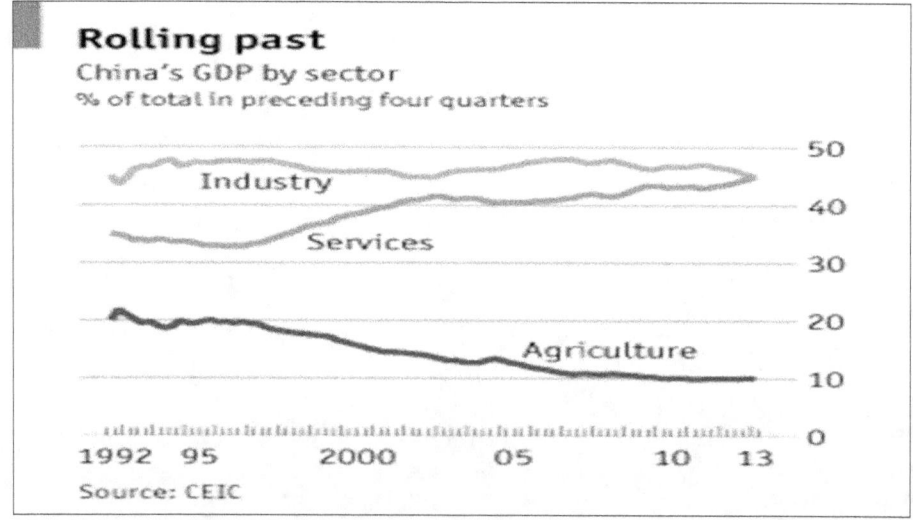

Rolling past

China's GDP by sector
% of total in preceding four quarters

Industry

Services

Agriculture

1992 95 2000 05 10 13

Source: CEIC

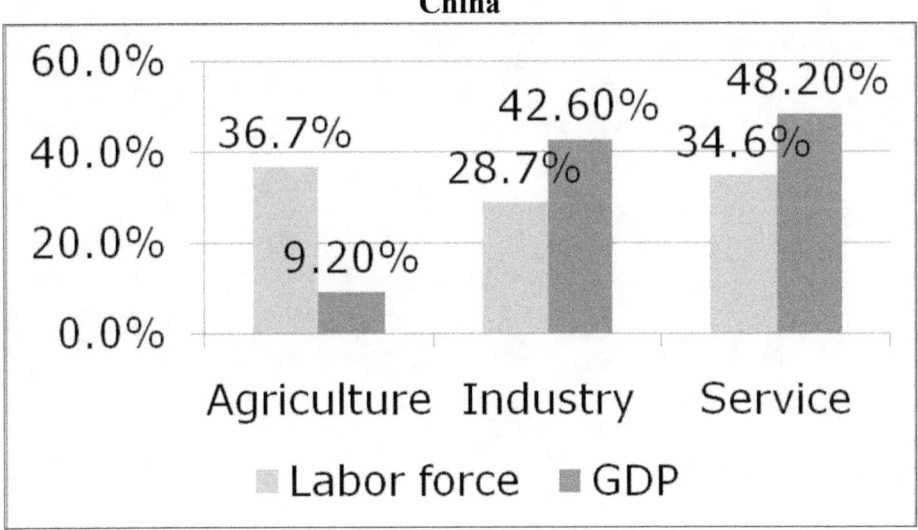

China

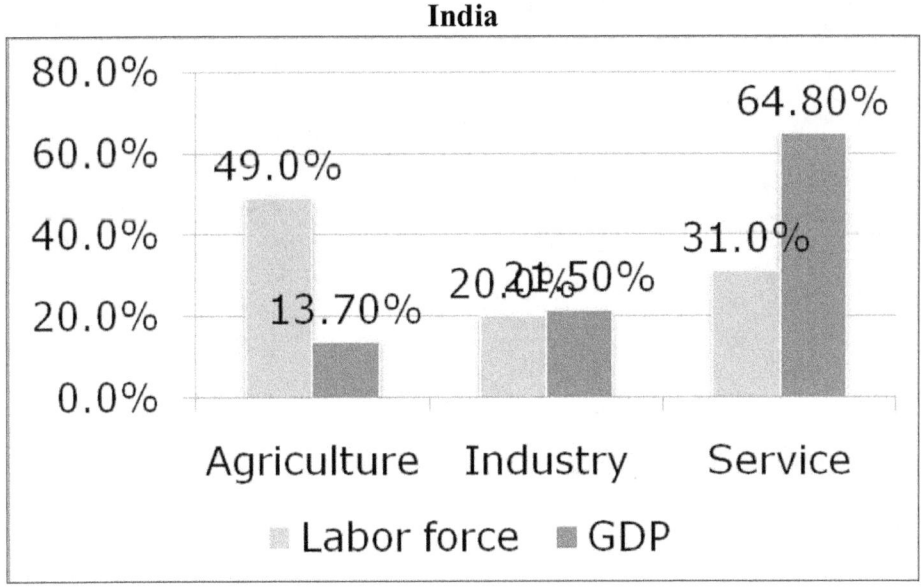

India

GDP Components

What's Driving Growth—China

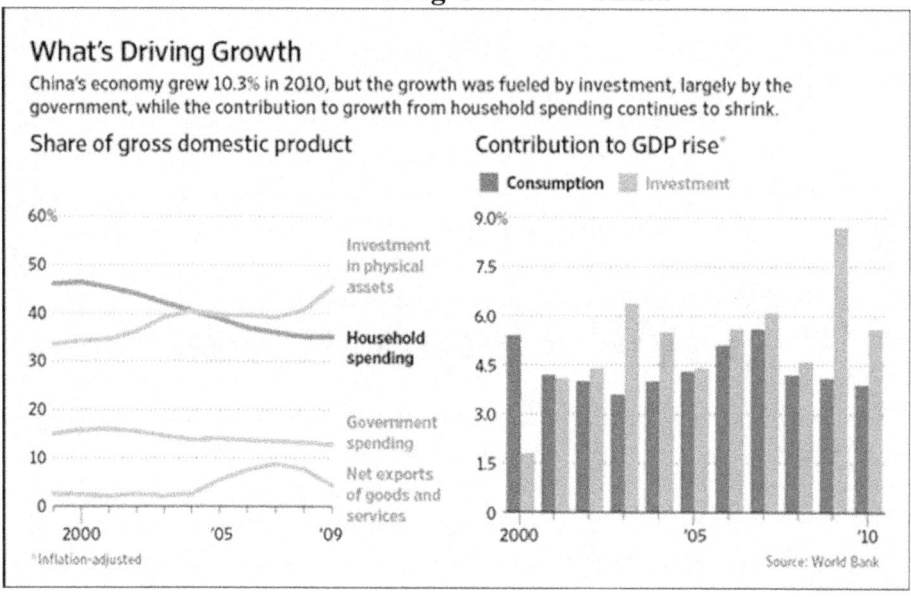

What's Driving Growth

China's economy grew 10.3% in 2010, but the growth was fueled by investment, largely by the government, while the contribution to growth from household spending continues to shrink.

Indian GDP Components

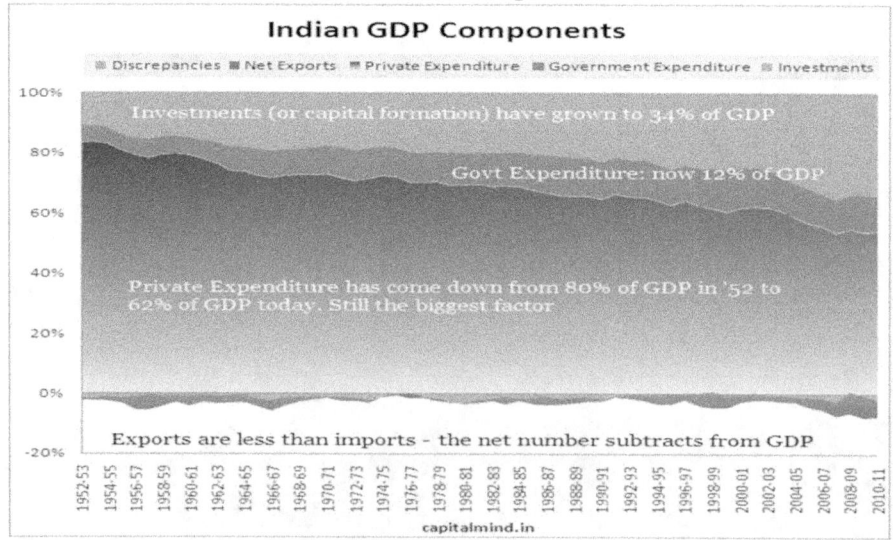

Can India Catch up with China?

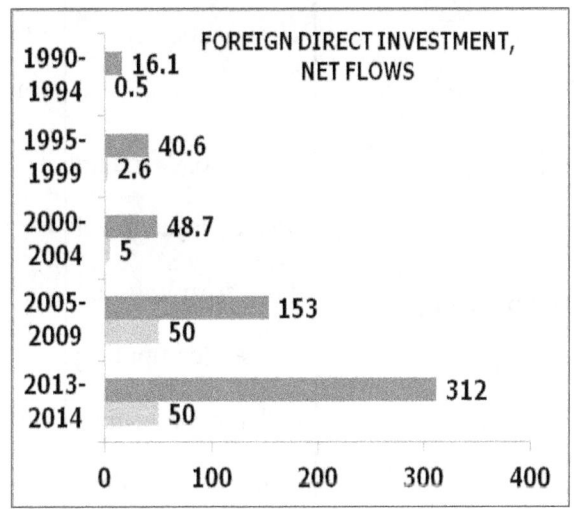

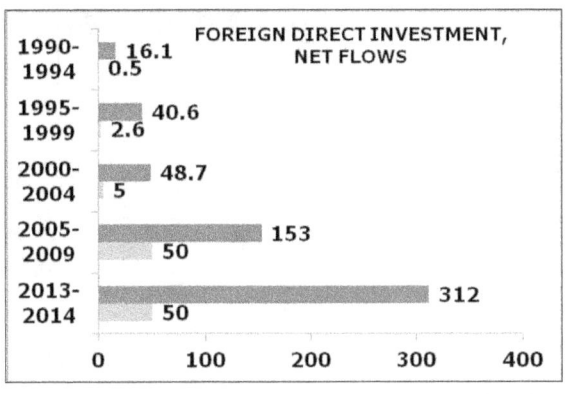

India Tops Economic Survey

Bull Run **Strong Economic Outlook** **Ranking (Country-wise)**		**85%** of firms in India reported revenues higher than last year. **74%** of firms expect to grow with improved economic sentiments. **44%** of Indian finance leaders feel that spending on cloud computing will form a critical component of their increased spending on technology.	Three out of every four Indian finance leaders feel that fresh spending and investments could help new business partnerships.
India	**94%**		
US	**83%**		
UK	**74%**		
Mexico	**73%**		
Singapore	**70%**		
Aggressive Spending and Investment			
India	**38%**		
China	**28%**		
US	**13%**		

Modest Hike in Outlay for Defence

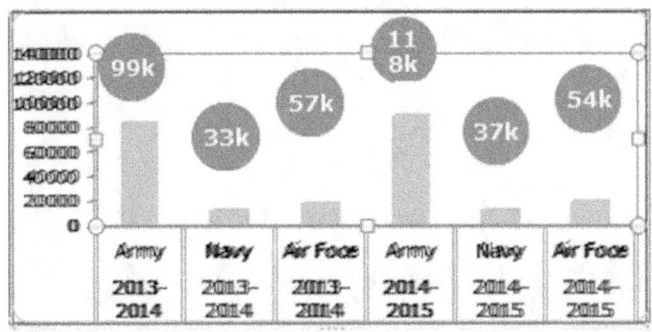

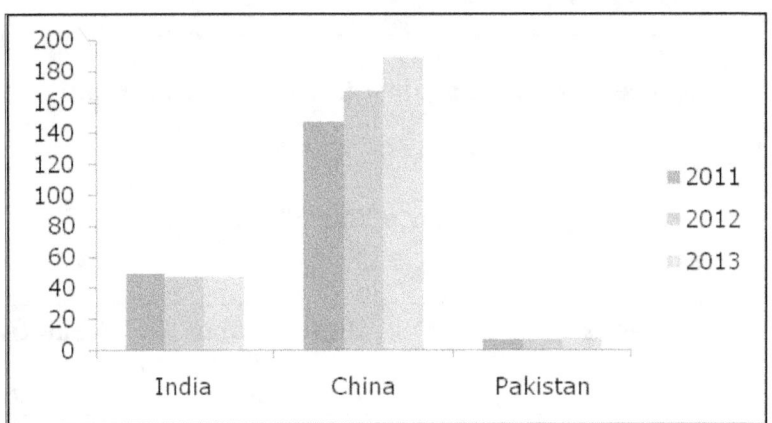

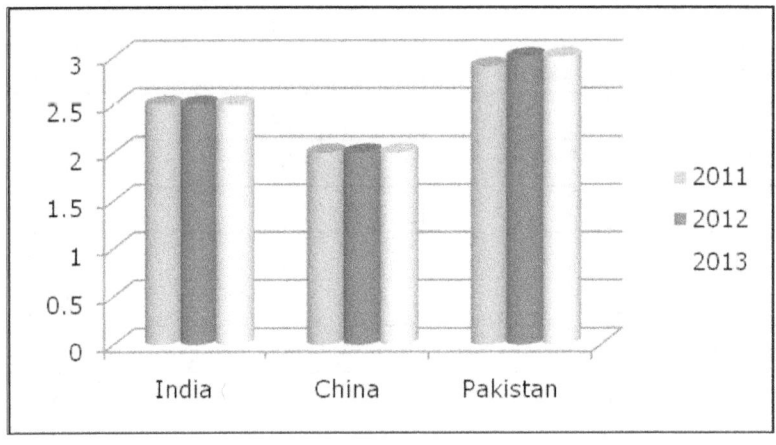

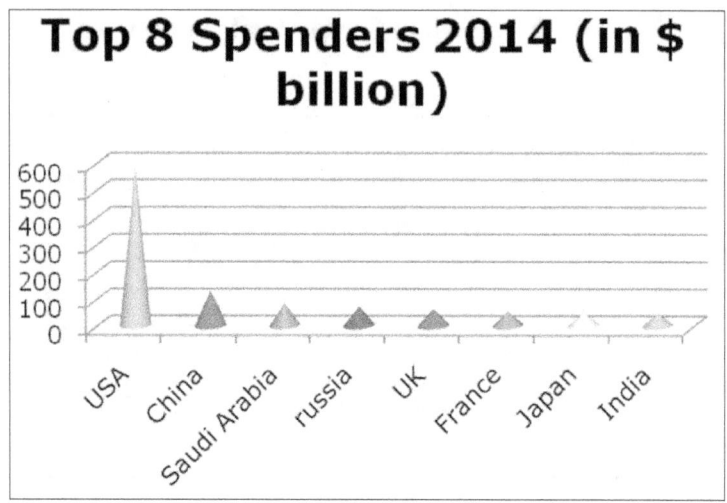

Rupee to Weaken against Dollar over One Year

Poised for a Poor Show

Banks	Rupee-dollar exchange Dec. 2015	Tentative targets Mar. 2016
SBI	64	64
Standard Chartered Bank	64	64
Deutsche Bank	64	64
Axis Bank	63.5	63.75
Yes Bank	63.5	63
Barclays	64.65	64.5
Kotak Mahindra	64	64.5
India Forex Advisors	64	64
Mecklai Financial	64.65	65.66
Kotak Securities	64	65
Edelweiss	65	64.5

Rupee Falls below 64 Dollars, Hits 20 Months' Low

Sliding Again **Why Did the** **Rupee Fall?**	VS $ (Inverted Scale) 100 54.15 68.83 64.24 7-May-13 Aug28 137-May
➢ Sale of Indian assets by foreign investors triggered weakness in the currency.	What will be the impact? ➢ Pressure on oil prices may result in pass-through to consumers.
➢ The rise in crude prices promoted oil cost to rush to the market to book crude oil, creating more demand for dollars.	➢ With foreign investors exiting, RBI will not be able to cut rates.
➢ Banks forecasting the rupee at 65 promoted exporters to delay selling dollars.	➢ Sales by foreign investors have resulted in yields on government bonds rising. This will prevent deposit rates from falling further.
➢ Compared to other emerging markets, the rupee had weakened the least against the dollar in FY15, and a correction was seen as inevitable.	➢ IT cos. exporters to get a boost— BSE-IT index rose 1.6% on Thursday.

Romancing the Dragon

PM Will Push China to Cut Trade Deficit

Great Wall of Imbalance

	2010–11	2011–12	2012–13	2013–14	2014–15
India's exports	14.2	18.1	13.5	14.8	10.9
India's imports	44.5	55.3	52.2	51	55.8
Trade deficit	30.3	37.2	38.7	36.2	44.9

Top Exports ($M)

	2013–14	2012–15
Cotton	3,833	2,074
Copper and products	1,841	1,740
Ores	1,571	491
Fuel, oil, etc.	1,022	1,223
Organic chemicals	919	904

Top Exports ($M)

	2013–14	2014–15
Electrical machinery	14,229	15,459
Nuclear reactors*	9,445	9,166
Organic chemicals	5,396	5,885
Iron, steel, and products	2,195	5,885
Fertilizers	1,926	2,962

Factors of Production

Technology

a. The growth of labour productivity is the key long-term determinant of the differences between economic performance in India and China and the extent to which income levels in these countries are catching up to those in the OECD area.

b. Prior to 1980, income growth was held back in both countries by adherence to socialist economic policies that adversely impacted productivity growth.

c. In India, income per head increased at a very slow pace in the thirty years after independence with the total factor productivity increasing by less than 17 per cent in the whole period.

d. In the same period, performance in China was even worse, with cumulative growth of TFP of less than 10 per cent.

e. Nonetheless, income per head in China rose more rapidly than in India thanks to greater capital accumulation.

Reforms

Economic Policy

a. Economic reforms in both countries led to significant improvement in economic performance from the 1980s onwards.

b. The growth of total factor productivity accelerated markedly in China and, though slowing in recent years, remains rapid.

c. Moving enterprises from the public sector to the private sector has been one factor behind the rapid growth of TFP, given the much higher level of TFP in private enterprises compared with public companies in China (Dougherty and Herd 2007).

d. Moreover, capital accumulation accelerated to an even greater extent.

e. In India, the improvements in both TFP and, especially, capital accumulation have been more modest.

f. The relatively low level of capital accumulation has meant that TFP growth in India has accounted for a much larger proportion of total labour productivity growth than in China, even though TFP growth has been slower in India than in China.

g. The movement of total factor productivity and capital formation are not, of course, independent. In particular, the combination of a rapid growth in TFP at the start of the reform period in China helped boost the growth of income and may have been one of the factors that led to the increase in the savings rate in the 1980s.

h. Reform in India has been much more hesitant than in China, leading to less improvement in TFP and a slower increase in savings and domestic investment.

Make in India -is an promotional campaign by government of india to encourage MNCS set up business in india offering favorable terms like free land, subsidised electric power, tax holidays.

Automobiles

- Domestic Markets Share, 2013–14

  1. Passenger vehicles—13.59 per cent

  2. Commercial vehicles—3.44 per cent

  3. Three-wheelers—2.60 per cent

  4. Two-wheelers—80.37 per cent

- The industry currently accounts for almost 7 per cent of the country's GDP and employs about 19 million people, both directly and indirectly.

- India is currently the seventh-largest producer in the world, with an average annual production of 17.5 million vehicles, of which 2.3 million are exported.

- The Indian automobile market is estimated to become the third largest in the world by 2016 and will account for more than 5 per cent of global vehicle sales.

- India is the second-largest two-wheeler manufacturer, the largest motorcycle manufacturer, and the fifth largest commercial vehicle manufacturer in the world.

- The total turnover in 2010–11 was USD 58.5 billion; turnover by 2016 is slated to be USD 145 billion.

Make in India

Defence

- India has the third-largest armed forces in the world.

- India is one of the largest importers of conventional defence equipment and spends about 40 per cent of its total defence budget on capital acquisitions.

- About 60 per cent of its defence requirements are met through imports.

- The allocation for defence in the last budget was approximately USD 37.3 billion.

Make in India

IT and Engineering

- IT-BPM revenue is expected to reach USD 118 billion in 2014.

- Exports from the IT-BPM industry are expected to reach USD 86.4 billion in 2014.

- IT services exports are USD 52 billion.

- Engineering and R and D services and software products exports are USD 14 billion. The hardware industry exports are USD 0.4 billion.

- The IT-BPM industry is the largest private sector employer— delivering 3.1 million jobs.

- The sector accounts for 38 per cent of India's services exports.

- The sector includes six hundred offshore development centres (ODCs) of seventy-eight countries.

Budget 2015

Rebooting India's Impact on Economy

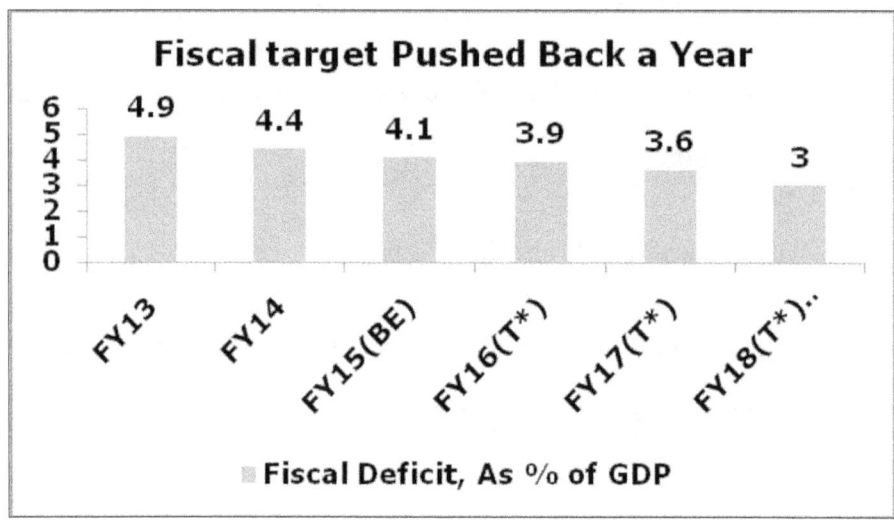

Fiscal target Pushed Back a Year

FY13	FY14	FY15(BE)	FY16(T*)	FY17(T*)	FY18(T*)
4.9	4.4	4.1	3.9	3.6	3

Fiscal Deficit, As % of GDP

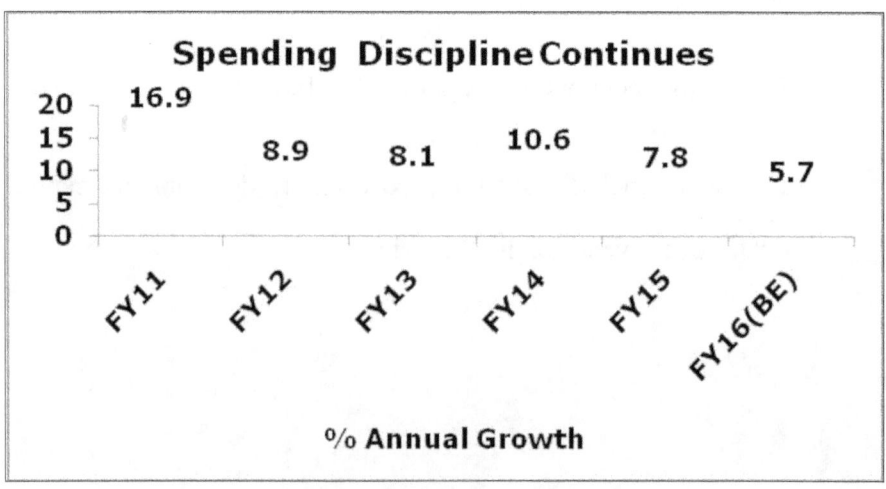

Spending Discipline Continues

FY11	FY12	FY13	FY14	FY15	FY16(BE)
16.9	8.9	8.1	10.6	7.8	5.7

% Annual Growth

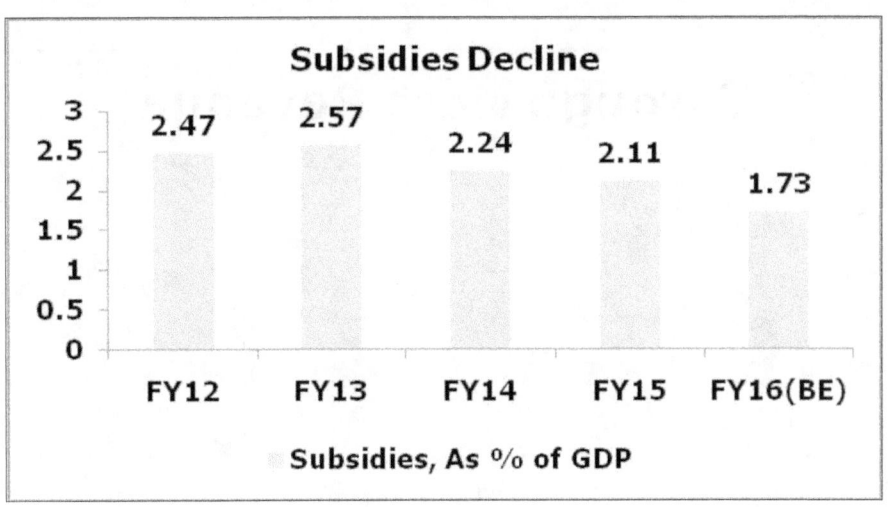

Budget 2015

Rebooting India's Impact on Economy

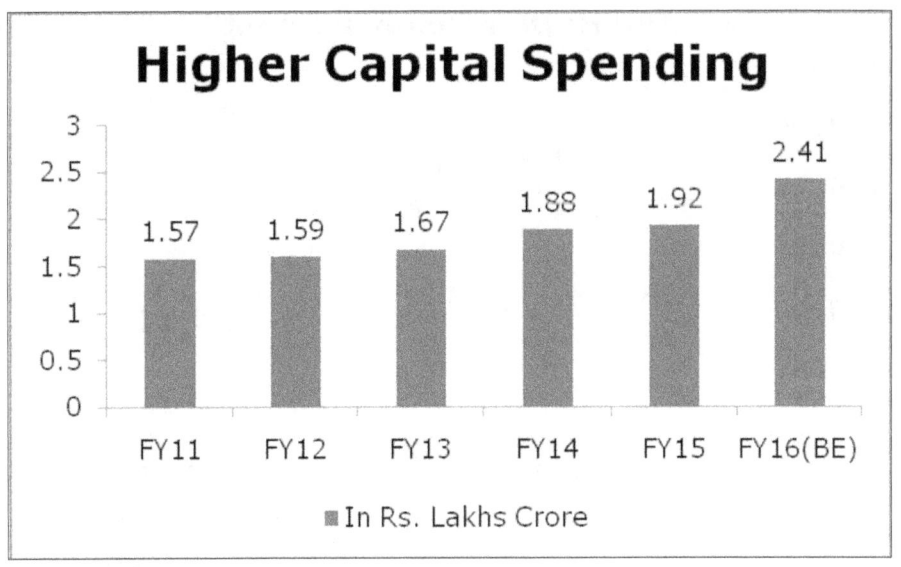

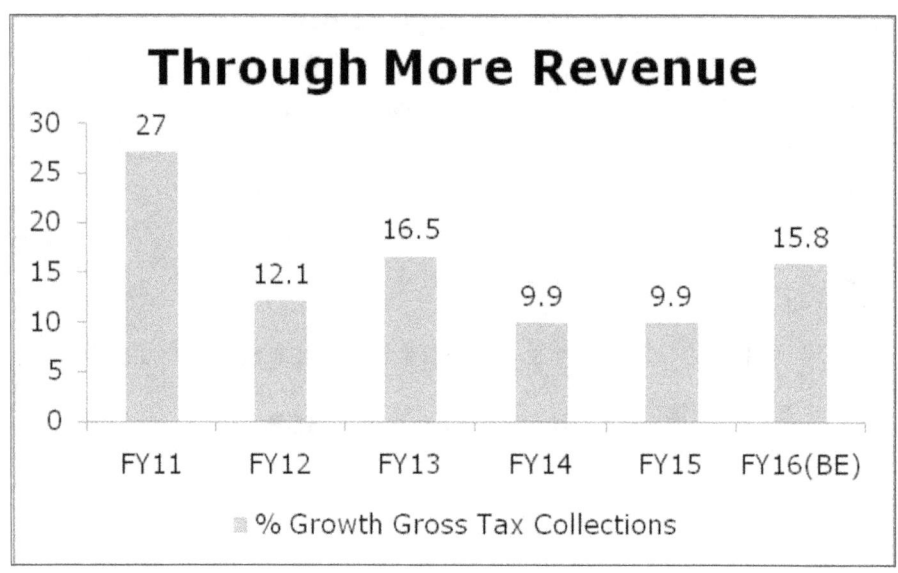

Through More Revenue

- FY11: 27
- FY12: 12.1
- FY13: 16.5
- FY14: 9.9
- FY15: 9.9
- FY16(BE): 15.8

% Growth Gross Tax Collections

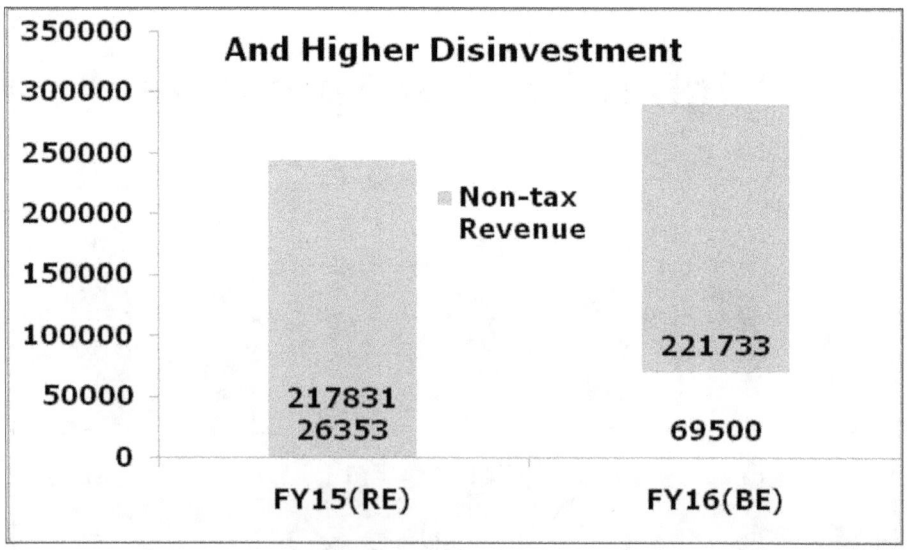

And Higher Disinvestment

Non-tax Revenue

- FY15(RE): 217831 / 26353
- FY16(BE): 221733 / 69500

What's Wrong with Oil?

Cheaper crude is hammering the Gulf, Russia, and Venezuela, while Asia is rejoicing in the price mayhem. There's more action in the offing.

The Oil Math

➢ Crude oil plunges to a six-year low at $45.89.

➢ Two weeks into the new year, benchmark crude prices have already plummeted more than 15 per cent.

➢ This is a potential threat to oil-exporting nations that rely solely on crude to power their economies.

➢ The oil price plunge slows down the rate of economic growth (stagflationary effect on macro economy of an oil-importing nation).

➢ A hike in oil price gives rise to inflation.

Why the Plunge

> ➤ A persistent mismatch between global supply and demand continues.

> ➤ Big oil producers, part of OPEC, are spooking markets by refusing to cut production to stem the price plunge (which leads to excess supply).

> ➤ A fraction of oil importers in Europe and the United States have cut down on oil consumption due to a renewed focus on shale gas.

What's Wrong with Oil?

Maximum Impact

> ➤ It is borne by petro economies like Russia, Gulf countries, and Venezuela, apart from OPEC members.

> ➤ Brent crude fell 50 per cent in the last four months.

> ➤ Sooner or later, United States production of oil may be shut down, leading to a cascading recessionary effect.

> ➤ OPEC members could suffer brain damage of the economy, which could be irreversible in the backdrop of muted recessionary signs in the overall global market.

> ➤ Russia was awarded 'junk' status by Fitch on Friday, meaning its economy is on the brink (Russia debts have become riskier).

> ➤ Venezuelan debt was downgraded to the second-lowest rating by Moodys).

Biggest Oil Producers

1. United States

2. Saudi Arabia

3. Russia

> We don't care. Even $20 a barrel won't trigger a change of heart.
>
> —Ali Al-Naimi, Saudi Arabia's oil minister

Divergent Thinking

Critical Success Factor

Any signs of government influence in the central bank's decisions would worry investors, given India's history of high spending, which, if accompanied by low interest rates, could lead to a surge in inflation and deepening debt problems.

Independence at Stake

How a Monetary Policy Committee in India Could Look

1. The government and the Reserve Bank of India (RBI) are set to consider proposals for the formation of a Monetary Policy Committee (MPC), which will take key decisions such as interest rate changes, but they have raised concerns over the central bank's independence.

2. There are two competing proposals to establish a MPC, one from an external panel appointed by the Finance Ministry and another from the Reserve Bank of India.

3. MPCs are a common feature in central banks globally.

Urban Revamp

Cabinet Clears Proposals Aimed at Driving Economic Growth

100 Cities to Turn Smart

Redrawing the Urban Landscape

Centre Approves Outlay of Nearly Rs. 1 Lakh Crore to Make Cities More Liveable

➤ Rs. 48,000 crore for smart cities mission

➤ One hundred smart cities to receive Rs. 100 crore per year for five years

➤ Rs. 50,000 crore for the Atal Mission for Rejuvenation and Urban Transformation

➤ Five hundred cities and towns with a population of one lakh and above to receive funds in three instalments

➤ Over Rs. 2 lakhs crore to flow into urban areas over the next five years

Raising Funds

➤ Special-purpose vehicle to be created for each city to implement a smart-city action plan

➤ Public–private partnership model to be used for local bodies to mobilize private investment

IMF Predicts India Will Hit 7.5% Growth, Overtake China

Positive Outlook
The IMF has forecast India's growth to strengthen from 7.2% in 2014 to 7.5% in 2016.

1. For the first time since 1999, India's growth rate may eclipse China's. 2. IMF chief economist, Oliver Blanchard, says there is increasing divergence in the growth paths of the two countries. 3. India is trying to shift from consumption to investment-led growth at a time when China is going the opposite way.	**GDP growth projections** 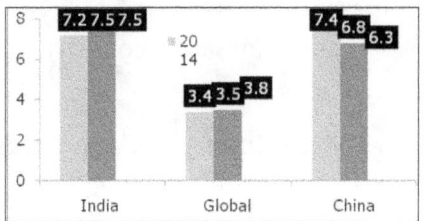

Strategic Fit and Best Fit Analysis

> ➤ India–US synergy—Encourage American MNCs to set up manufacturing and IT bases in India.

> ➤ Focus on parts export, graduate to products, set up the value change, improve pricing, and provide value to customers. Build and maintain a competitive advantage.

> ➤ Place Indian workmen in America for their product and service support.

> ➤ China is changing the world in its unique way. It is now on the part of Superdome. It is building Lebensraum in the South China Sea.

> ➤ The one road, one belt push into Central Asia and beyond Europe—influence to reach, and strategies, drinking sixty-five countries and four billion people in its am bit.

> ➤ Maintaining a good relationship with America in the West and China in the East with the policy of "American quality, Chinese pricing" will be the best strategic fit.

> ➤ India has to focus on its biggest strength of having fertile land and considerable manpower in rural India to develop the agriculture segment.

The author is an engineer and a charted financial analyst with twenty-six years of successful work experience with MNCs. The author is an alumnus of BITS Pilani and the Indian Institute of Management, Trichy.